A·C·T·I·O·N B·O·O·K

DISCOVER THE TITANIC

Eric Kentley

DK PUBLISHING, INC.

A DK PUBLISHING BOOK

Project Editor Claire Bampton
Senior Editor Sue Leonard
US Editor Camela Decaire
Art Editors Jane Bull, Cathy Chesson
Picture Researcher Tom Worsley
Photographer Steve Gorton
Paper Engineer David Hawcock

Illustrator Hans Jenssen

Managing Editor Sarah Phillips
Senior Managing Art Editor Peter Bailey
DTP Designers Karen Nettelfield, Andrew O'Brien
Design Assistant Miranda May
Production Joanne Blackmore, Lauren Britton

First American Edition, 1997

4 6 8 10 9 7 5 3

Published in the United States by
DK Publishing, Inc.
95 Madison Avenue
New York, New York 10016

Visit us on the World Wide Web at http://www.dk.com

Copyright © 1997 Dorling Kindersley Limited, London

Published in Great Britain by Dorling Kindersley Limited

A catalog record is available from the Library of Congress.

ISBN: 0-7894-2020-1

Color reproduction by Flying Colours, Italy
Manufactured in China for Imago

Security clearance

This is your identity card. Access to the site of the wreck is strictly
controlled, so please fill in your details and attach a photograph of
yourself in the space provided.
Present it to the security staff
at Ponta Delgada quayside.
They will allow you to board
the research vessel *Nadir*, and
join the expedition to the
wreck of the *Titanic*.

During the
expedition you
should display your
badge at all times.

Titanic Recovery
Expeditions

Please glue a
photograph of
yourself here.

Name *Stephanie S.*

Age *12*

Height *5'2"*

Signature *Stephanie Joyce*

Explorer's tasks

Your expedition is divided into three stages: the trip out to the
site of the wreck on the *Nadir*, a tour around the *Titanic* in
Nautile, and raising and restoring objects from the wreck for
display in an exhibition. For each stage you will have an
expedition leader who will set you a number of explorer's tasks.
Work through the tasks carefully on a separate piece of paper.
You can then check whether your answers are correct on page 30.

The *Nadir*
and *Nautile*

Titanic Recovery Expeditions

Congratulations! You have been successful in your application to visit the wreck of the most famous ship in the world, the *Titanic*. Your expedition will start at the quayside at Ponta Delgada, in the Azores. There you will set sail, on the *Nadir*, and travel to the spot where the *Titanic* sank more than 85 years ago. You will then descend in a submersible (small submarine) called *Nautile* to the seabed, where the wreck lies. After a tour of the *Titanic*, you will recover some objects from the site of the wreck. Back on board the *Nadir*, you will learn how to restore them for display in an exhibition intended to keep the legend of the *Titanic* alive. Three experienced expedition leaders will tell you about the *Titanic* and help you during your voyage.

Enjoy yourself – and "bon voyage"!

ITINERARY

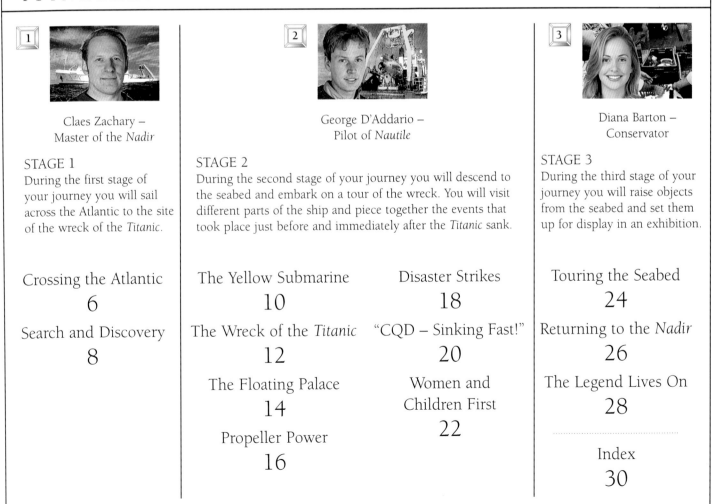

Claes Zachary –
Master of the *Nadir*

George D'Addario –
Pilot of *Nautile*

Diana Barton –
Conservator

STAGE 1
During the first stage of your journey you will sail across the Atlantic to the site of the wreck of the *Titanic*.

STAGE 2
During the second stage of your journey you will descend to the seabed and embark on a tour of the wreck. You will visit different parts of the ship and piece together the events that took place just before and immediately after the *Titanic* sank.

STAGE 3
During the third stage of your journey you will raise objects from the seabed and set them up for display in an exhibition.

Crossing the Atlantic

"Hello and welcome on board. I'm Claes Zachary, the master of the research vessel *Nadir*. I'm going to tell you where we're going, and how we will get there."

■ The *Titanic's* doomed voyage began at Southampton, England, on Wednesday, April 10, 1912. After stopping at Cherbourg, France, and Queenstown, Ireland, the *Titanic* set out across the Atlantic Ocean the following day, scheduled to reach New York seven days later. She sank in the early hours of April 15. Sailing in the *Nadir* it will take us four and a half days to reach the spot where the *Titanic* sank.

The *Nadir* and *Nautile*
The *Nadir* is the vessel that will carry the submersible *Nautile* to the site of the wreck. She has a crew of 15, but she also carries 14 people to maintain and staff *Nautile*. This leaves space for ten other expedition members, including you.

Ocean liners
Before passenger planes were available, many shipping firms ran services across the Atlantic. The *Titanic*, owned by the White Star Line, carried passengers and mail and so was called the RMS (Royal Mail Steamer) *Titanic*.

THE FATEFUL VOYAGE
When the *Titanic* was completed in 1912, she was the largest and, for the first-class passengers, the most luxurious ship in the world. Thought to be unsinkable, the *Titanic* sank on her maiden (first) voyage. Hundreds died, including some of the world's richest people.

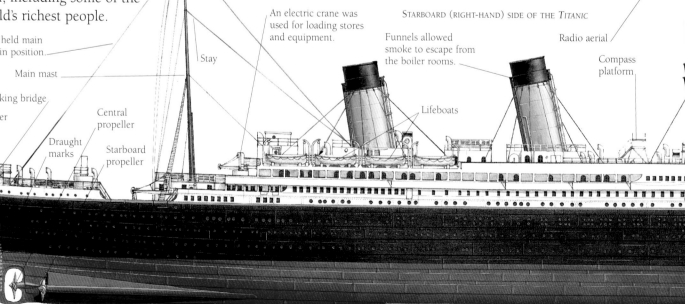

Stays held main mast in position.

Main mast

Docking bridge

Rudder

Draught marks

Central propeller

Starboard propeller

Stay

An electric crane was used for loading stores and equipment.

STARBOARD (RIGHT-HAND) SIDE OF THE *TITANIC*

Funnels allowed smoke to escape from the boiler rooms.

Lifeboats

Radio aerial

Compass platform

Navigating Across the Atlantic

In 1912, ships like the *Titanic* used a combination of speed, compass, clock, and astronomical observations to estimate their position. Modern ships record their position using degrees longitude, which measure how far east or west they are, and degrees latitude, which show how far north or south they are. At the North Pole (90° N) the North Star is almost directly overhead.

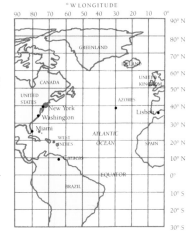

TASK 1

If a ship starts out from 30° W, 40° N, where is it leaving?

TASK 2

The ship sails along the same line of latitude until it reaches 76° W. Where is it?

TASK 3

The ship sails again, this time until it reaches 40° W and 20° S. Can its passengers see the North Star?

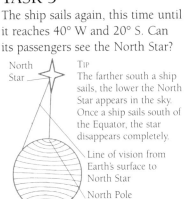

TIP
The farther south a ship sails, the lower the North Star appears in the sky. Once a ship sails south of the Equator, the star disappears completely.

North Star

Line of vision from Earth's surface to North Star

North Pole

Earth

Lines of latitude

ROUTES ACROSS THE ATLANTIC

The *Titanic* traveled faster than we will in the *Nadir*. She took less than three and a half days to travel from Queenstown to the point where she sank. The route the *Titanic* took was often used in the cold months to avoid the worst ice fields and icebergs.

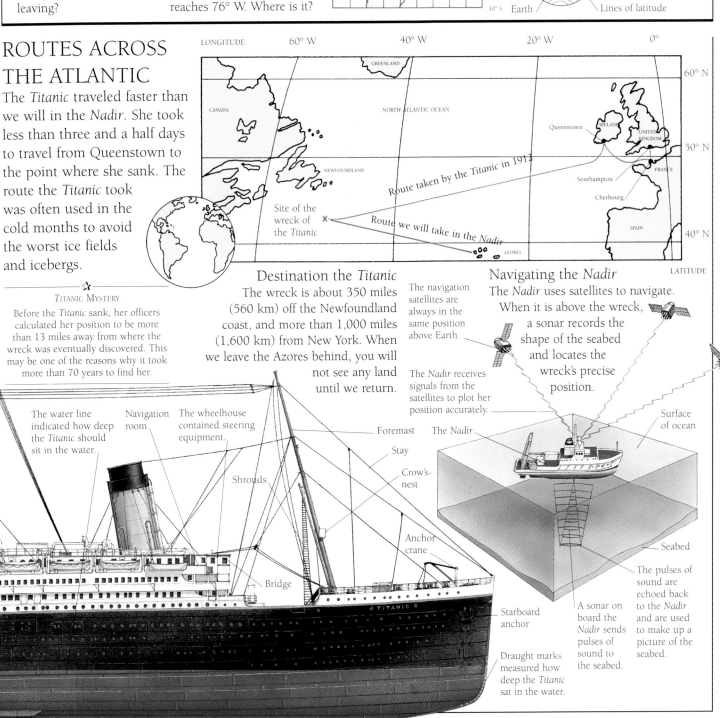

☆
TITANIC MYSTERY

Before the *Titanic* sank, her officers calculated her position to be more than 13 miles away from where the wreck was eventually discovered. This may be one of the reasons why it took more than 70 years to find her.

LONGITUDE 60° W 40° W 20° W 0°

GREENLAND

CANADA

NORTH ATLANTIC OCEAN

60° N

NEWFOUNDLAND

Route taken by the Titanic in 1912

Queenstown IRELAND UNITED KINGDOM 50° N

FRANCE

Southampton

Cherbourg

Site of the wreck of the *Titanic*

Route we will take in the *Nadir*

SPAIN 40° N

AZORES

LATITUDE

Destination the *Titanic*

The wreck is about 350 miles (560 km) off the Newfoundland coast, and more than 1,000 miles (1,600 km) from New York. When we leave the Azores behind, you will not see any land until we return.

The navigation satellites are always in the same position above Earth.

The *Nadir* receives signals from the satellites to plot her position accurately.

Navigating the *Nadir*

The *Nadir* uses satellites to navigate. When it is above the wreck, a sonar records the shape of the seabed and locates the wreck's precise position.

The water line indicated how deep the *Titanic* should sit in the water.

Navigation room

The wheelhouse contained steering equipment.

Foremast

The *Nadir*

Surface of ocean

Stay

Crow's-nest

Shrouds

Anchor crane

Seabed

Bridge

Starboard anchor

Draught marks measured how deep the *Titanic* sat in the water.

A sonar on board the *Nadir* sends pulses of sound to the seabed.

The pulses of sound are echoed back to the *Nadir* and are used to make up a picture of the seabed.

TITANIC

Search and Discovery

■ We are now directly above where the wreck of the *Titanic* lies on the seabed. Immediately after the disaster, people talked about recovering the *Titanic*, but even if she had been located, the technology to reach her was not available. The tools necessary for deep-sea exploration were developed only in the late 1970s. It was then that the search for the *Titanic* began in earnest.

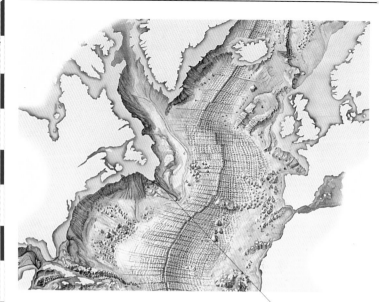

The Atlantic Ocean
The natural features of the mid-Atlantic seabed are a complicated mixture of hills, plains, and valleys. The greatest depth is 28,681 ft (8,742 m).

The *Titanic* was found at a depth of 12,460 ft (3,798 m) at the base of a continental shelf.

A continental shelf is a shallow area next to land.

Base of continental shelf

Site of the sunken wreck of the *Titanic*

EXPLORING THE SEABED

In 1985 Dr. Robert Ballard led a successful American/French expedition to find the *Titanic*. In two months the research ships *Le Suroit* and the *Knorr* surveyed over 100 square miles (260 square km) of Atlantic seabed using sonar and an unmanned submersible called *Argo*.

Underwater navigation

Signals from satellites, used for navigation on the surface, cannot be picked up underwater. Submersibles like *Argo* use underwater transponders that fix their position with the main ship. A submersible can then send out and receive signals from the transponders to plot its position.

The *Knorr*'s position was "fixed" by satellites.

A fiber cable sent information to and from *Argo* and the *Knorr*.

Specially designed propellers enabled the *Knorr* to hold its position in the water.

Transponder

Argo used a sonar system and video cameras to build up a picture of the seabed.

Three transponders were placed underwater to enable *Argo* to plot her precise position.

Transponder

A sonar receiver attached to the bottom of the *Knorr* allowed the transponders to plot their positions.

THE *KNORR*/*ARGO* TRANSPONDER NET

High flyer

Here *Argo* is being launched from the *Knorr*. *Argo* is a remote-controlled deep-towed deep-sea video vehicle. This unmanned submersible was connected to the *Knorr* by a very long fiber cable.

FLYING *ARGO* TO FIND THE *TITANIC*

Remote control
A pilot "flew" *Argo* with a joystick from the safety of the *Knorr*'s control room.

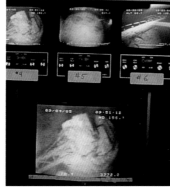

Filming the seabed
Argo's video cameras sent forward, down, and enlarged views of the seabed to the *Knorr*.

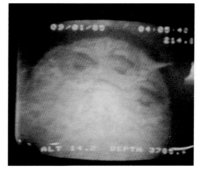

The *Titanic* found
At 1 a.m., on September 1, 1985, *Argo*'s pilot saw this image on the video monitor. It is the front of one of the *Titanic*'s boilers. Ballard's team had found the wreck!

The real thing
It was one of these boilers that was spotted by *Argo*'s video cameras.

The *Atlantis II* carried *Alvin* out to the site of the sinking.

Touring the *Titanic*
On July 13, 1986, Ballard returned to the site of the wreck to make the first manned dive to the sunken *Titanic*. He did this in a submersible called *Alvin*.

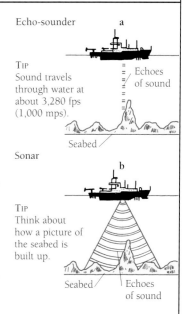

Alvin was launched from the stern of the *Atlantis II*.

☆

TITANIC MYSTERY

Ballard's team spotted the first sign of the *Titanic* wreckage at 1 a.m. on September 1, 1985. The British newspaper *The Observer* announced the story the same day. Because of the different time zones this means the story must have been printed at least eight hours before the discovery was made! Did someone know where the *Titanic* was all the time?

The robotic eye
Alvin can take three people to the seabed. It can also carry *Jason Junior*, a remote-controlled robot that can explore inside the wreck. The small robot is piloted from inside *Alvin*. It carries its own lights, still camera, and video camera to record the wreck.

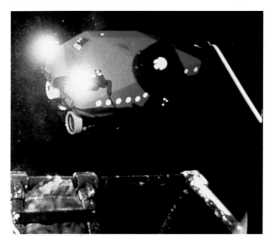

⚑ EXPLORER'S TASK ⓑ

Finding the *Titanic*
To help locate the *Titanic*, Ballard used both an echo-sounder and a sonar. He used an echo-sounder to measure the depth of the sea, and a sonar to build up pictures of the seabed. An echo-sounder beams a pulse of sound down to the seabed, where it is reflected just like an echo. Sonars work in the same way, but send out fan-shaped beams of sound.

TASK 1
In diagram **a**, if the echo is picked up six seconds after being sent, how deep is the water? a) 19,684 ft (6,000 m) b) 9,842 ft (3,000 m) c) 196,848 ft (60,000 m)

TASK 2
In diagram **b**, would all the echoes from the seabed arrive at the same time? Why?

Echo-sounder   a

TIP
Sound travels through water at about 3,280 fps (1,000 mps).

Echoes of sound

Seabed

Sonar   b

TIP
Think about how a picture of the seabed is built up.

Seabed   Echoes of sound

The Yellow Submarine

"Hello, I'm George D'Addario, pilot of *Nautile*. As we dive, I'll tell you how *Nautile* works. Then, when we reach the seabed, I'll guide you around the most famous wreck in the world."

■ Once we have boarded *Nautile*, she is taken to the stern (back end) of the *Nadir*, where a specially designed crane will swing her out and release her into the water. *Nautile* then drops down 12,460 ft (3,798 m) to the seabed. Our descent takes an hour and a half, but after the first few minutes it will be too dark to see anything. Use the bathroom before we leave – you will not get another chance for 11 hours!

Dropping off

As *Nautile* descends you will hardly notice any movement. During the dive, *Nautile* navigates by receiving signals from the *Nadir* and from transponders in the water around the wreck. She sends pictures to the *Nadir* through her own transmitter.

Keeping watch

Nautile carries three people: the pilot, the copilot, and yourself. When you reach the seabed keep a careful watch through your porthole – there is always the danger of hitting the wreck.

NAUTILE

Submersibles like *Nautile* are small submarines that can only work underwater for a few hours. *Nautile* has a top speed of 1.7 knots (2 mph/3 kph). Her thrusters and hinged propeller make her highly maneuverable.

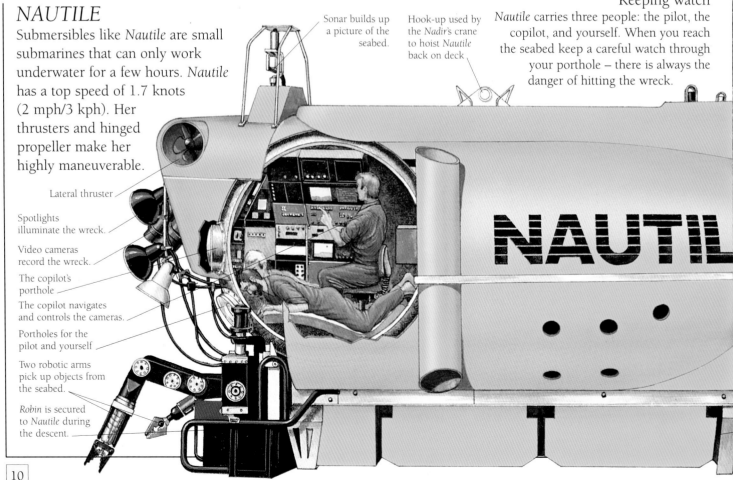

Sonar builds up a picture of the seabed.

Hook-up used by the *Nadir*'s crane to hoist *Nautile* back on deck

Lateral thruster

Spotlights illuminate the wreck.

Video cameras record the wreck.

The copilot's porthole

The copilot navigates and controls the cameras.

Portholes for the pilot and yourself

Two robotic arms pick up objects from the seabed.

Robin is secured to *Nautile* during the descent.

NAUTIL

Sink or swim

Before you descend, *Nautile*'s technicians will ask you your weight. This is because they must fill the ballast bags to the right weight so that *Nautile* will sink to the seabed. The bags are filled with steel shot and will be left on the seabed.

Powerful spotlight

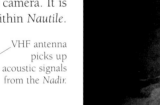

Video cameras

Portholes

Lights, cameras, action

The wreck of the *Titanic* is so deep that natural light could never reach it. So *Nautile* must take powerful spotlights with her. *Nautile* also carries one fixed and one movable video camera, which run constantly once she reaches the seabed.

Robin

To film inside the wreck, *Nautile* can carry *Robin*, a tethered and remote-controlled video camera. It is operated from within *Nautile*.

Acoustic head used for navigation

VHF antenna picks up acoustic signals from the *Nadir*.

Lateral thruster

Nautile carries enough oxygen to last five days underwater in case of an emergency.

Hinged propeller

Echo-sounder charts depth of water.

Main batteries power *Nautile* for 12 hours.

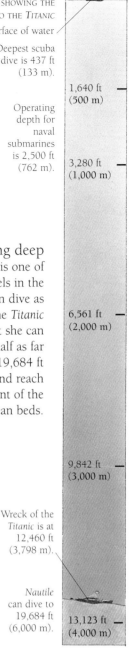

SCALE ILLUSTRATION SHOWING THE *NADIR* IN RELATION TO THE *TITANIC*

Surface of water

Deepest scuba dive is 437 ft (133 m).

1,640 ft (500 m)

Operating depth for naval submarines is 2,500 ft (762 m).

3,280 ft (1,000 m)

Diving deep

Nautile is one of the few vessels in the world that can dive as deep as the *Titanic* wreck. In fact she can dive almost half as far again, to 19,684 ft (6,000 m) and reach 97 percent of the world's ocean beds.

6,561 ft (2,000 m)

9,842 ft (3,000 m)

Wreck of the *Titanic* is at 12,460 ft (3,798 m).

Nautile can dive to 19,684 ft (6,000 m).

13,123 ft (4,000 m)

⭐ EXPLORER'S TASK (C)

Navigating underwater

Transponders are placed, using satellite navigation, around the wreck of the *Titanic*. Sound signals from *Nautile* are picked up by the transponders, which immediately send back a sound signal. By figuring out how far away each transponder is, *Nautile*'s computers calculate her position.

Surface of water

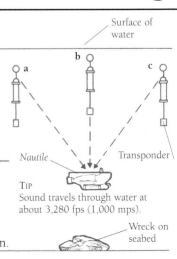

b

a

c

Nautile

Transponder

TASK 1

Nautile receives a signal from transponder **a** after two seconds, transponder **b** one second later, and transponder **c** after another second. Figure out how far away transponders **a**, **b**, and **c** are from *Nautile* so that the computer can plot your position.

TIP
Sound travels through water at about 3,280 fps (1,000 mps).

Wreck on seabed

The Wreck of the *Titanic*

■ *Nautile* will land on the seabed some distance from the wreck to avoid any possibility of damage. We will switch on her spotlights and travel over the bottom until you get your first view of the *Titanic* – of her bow, which plowed into the the seabed. The range of the spotlights is not very great, so your view will be limited. Lie down flat, look out of your porthole, and get ready to begin the tour.

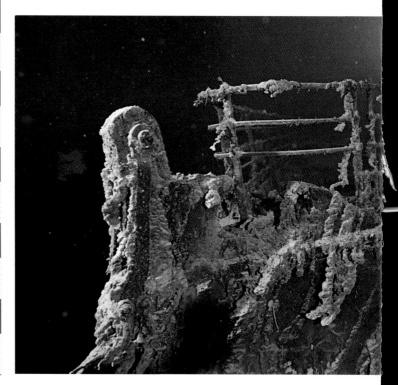

BELFAST GIANT

The *Titanic* and her sister ship, the *Olympic,* were built in Belfast in Ireland, at the Harland and Wolff shipyard. The *Titanic's* first keel plate was laid on March 31, 1909. On May 31, 1911, she was launched, but as an empty shell. The interior was then completed and she was finally ready for sea trials by the end of March 1912. More than 11,300 workers helped build the *Titanic*.

Your first glimpse

If you look ahead, you will see the huge bow of the *Titanic* towering over us. As we rise you will notice that rivers of "rust" cascade down her sides, covering her name.

Building the *Titanic*

Three hundred and fifty steel frames, with ten levels of deck supports, formed the skeleton of the *Titanic*. Steel plates, up to 6 ft (1.8 m) high, 36 ft (11 m) wide, and weighing 4.96 tons (4.5 tonnes) were riveted to the frames.

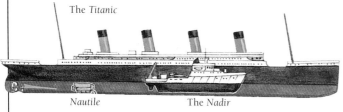

The *Titanic*

Nautile   The *Nadir*

Comparing sizes

This diagram shows the size of the *Titanic* in comparison to the *Nadir* and *Nautile*. The *Titanic* was 883 ft (269 m) long, *Nadir* is 184 ft (56 m) long, and *Nautile* is just 26 ft (8 m) long. The *Titanic* was 34 times longer than *Nautile*.

Touring the wreck

When the *Titanic* sank, she split in half. This model shows the bow section of the wreck. We will be exploring both halves during our tour.

The *Titanic* broke into two sections between her third and fourth funnels.

How ships float

If you drop a solid piece of steel into water, it sinks. So how can a huge ship float? The answer is that because a ship's hull is hollow, the weight of water it displaces is more than the weight of ship and cargo. The weight of this displaced water leads to an upthrust, or force, which makes the ship seem lighter in the water.

TASK 1

The *Titanic* weighed 50,706 tons (46,000 tonnes) and displaced 66,139 tons (60,000 tonnes) of water. The *Nadir* weighs 1,080 tons (980 tonnes) and displaces 2,232 tons (2,025 tonnes) of water. Look at diagrams **a** and **b**, which give two options for the *Titanic*, and **c**, which relates to the *Nadir*, and work out whether, once crew, passengers, and cargo have been added, the ships would float or sink.

The *Titanic* **a**

Crew, passengers, and cargo weigh 22,046 tons (20,000 tonnes)

The *Titanic* **b**

Crew, passengers, and cargo weigh 11,023 tons (10,000 tonnes)

The *Nadir* **c**

Crew, passengers, and cargo weigh 1,102 tons (1,000 tonnes)

Anchoring the ship

All of the *Titanic's* bow anchors are still in place. Such a large vessel needed three anchors to moor it. The 17-ton (15.5-tonne) center anchor lies here, useless, on the forecastle deck.

Spick and span

This is how the anchor looked in 1912. The chains were attached to the port (left-hand) and starboard (right-hand) anchors.

The debris field is approximately 1 mile (2.6 km) square.

★
TITANIC MYSTERY

Analysis of the steel of the *Titanic* has revealed a high sulfur content. In cold water, such as that found in the mid-Atlantic on the night of April 14, 1912, this could have made the *Titanic's* steel hull plates brittle. Could the quality of the steel have contributed to the sinking of the ship?

Gymnasium roof

Davit for lowering lifeboats

Remains of the foremast

Stern of wreck

Coal from the *Titanic's* boiler rooms

Debris field

Bow of wreck

MAP SHOWING THE SITE OF THE *TITANIC'S* WRECK

Our tour plan

During our tour we will be visiting various parts of the wreck of the *Titanic*. We will tour the public areas (A), the engines and boiler rooms (B), the crow's nest and the bow (C), the bridge (D), the upper deck (E), and the debris field (F).

Bunker hatch for coal

Anchor crane

Anchor

The Floating Palace

■ As we move around the wreck in *Nautile*, look carefully for the signs that show how magnificent the *Titanic* was in 1912. Deep within the ship lie the remains of spacious dining rooms, luxurious staterooms, elegant cafés, libraries, Turkish baths, a swimming pool, a gymnasium, and even a barbershop. On the *Titanic*, the accommodations for some passengers were more comfortable than their own homes!

ALL ABOARD

During the voyage, the *Titanic* was kept in good running order by an extensive crew. Captain Smith was in command of the 891 crew members. He had been a White Star captain for 25 years. This was to be his final voyage before retiring.

Captain Smith

Manning the ship

The ship's crew members were divided into three departments: the Deck Department of 73 people, including officers and seamen; the Engine Department of 325; and the Steward's Department of 494.

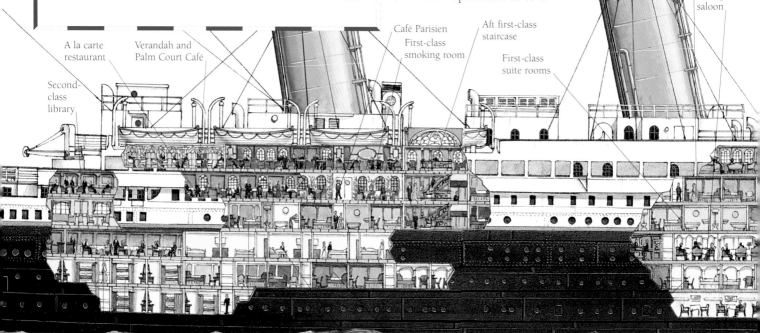

A la carte restaurant
Verandah and Palm Court Café
Second-class library
Café Parisien
First-class smoking room
Aft first-class staircase
First-class suite rooms
First-class staterooms
First-class dining saloon

Second-class dining room
Second-class cabins
First-class suite rooms
Hospital
First-class staterooms
Saloon bar
First-class staterooms

This deck bench is from one of the ship's promenades.

Seating at the stern
All three classes were kept separate. This promenade was where the third-class passengers could sit and relax or go for a stroll.

This gold-plated light fixture still hangs in place in the entrance hall.

Reading lights
Electric lights illuminated the first-class reading and writing room. This room was mainly used by women, unlike the smoking room, which was reserved for men.

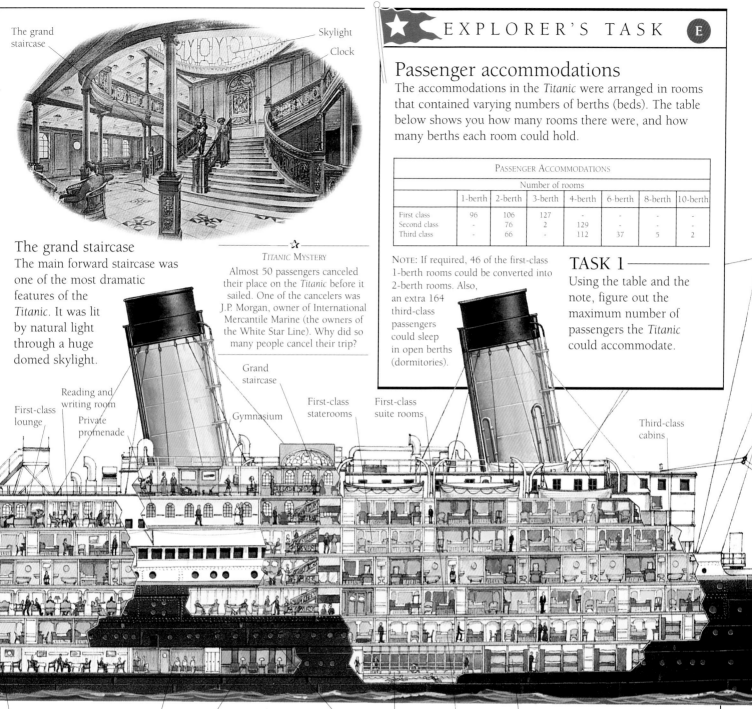

The grand staircase — Skylight — Clock

The grand staircase
The main forward staircase was one of the most dramatic features of the *Titanic*. It was lit by natural light through a huge domed skylight.

☆
TITANIC MYSTERY

Almost 50 passengers canceled their place on the *Titanic* before it sailed. One of the cancelers was J.P. Morgan, owner of International Mercantile Marine (the owners of the White Star Line). Why did so many people cancel their trip?

Passenger accommodations
The accommodations in the *Titanic* were arranged in rooms that contained varying numbers of berths (beds). The table below shows you how many rooms there were, and how many berths each room could hold.

PASSENGER ACCOMMODATIONS							
Number of rooms							
	1-berth	2-berth	3-berth	4-berth	6-berth	8-berth	10-berth
First class	96	106	127	-	-	-	-
Second class	-	76	2	129	-	-	-
Third class	-	66	-	112	37	5	2

NOTE: If required, 46 of the first-class 1-berth rooms could be converted into 2-berth rooms. Also, an extra 164 third-class passengers could sleep in open berths (dormitories).

TASK 1
Using the table and the note, figure out the maximum number of passengers the *Titanic* could accommodate.

First-class lounge
Reading and writing room
Private promenade
Gymnasium
Grand staircase
First-class staterooms
First-class suite rooms
Third-class cabins

Third-class dining saloon
Sauna and steam room
Turkish baths
First-class reception room
Swimming pool
First-class staterooms
Third-class cabins

This leaded window is from the first-class dining saloon.

The Captain's table
Captain Smith would dine with passengers at a table for six in the first-class dining saloon. The dining saloon could seat more than 500 people.

These windows look into one of the first-class rooms.

Traveling in style
The first-class rooms were large and luxurious. A first-class passenger paid about ten times as much as a third-class passenger.

Propeller Power

■ We will now leave the bow section of the *Titanic* and make the 1.5-mile (2.4-km) journey to the stern section. Here you will see the heart of the ship – the machinery that pushed her through the water. The *Titanic* was a triple-screw steamer. This means that she had three screws, or propellers, all powered by steam. Once you see one of the propellers you will begin to realize what an enormous ship the *Titanic* was.

POWERING THE *TITANIC*

The *Titanic* had two types of engines: a turbine engine and four reciprocating engines. Steam was produced in the six boiler rooms and piped to the engine rooms. The reciprocating engines turned the port and starboard propellers and the turbine powered the central propeller. Once it had passed through the engines, the steam was piped to the condensers where it cooled back into water, which could be used again.

CUTAWAY OF THE *TITANIC* SHOWING ENGINES AND BOILER ROOMS

Port propeller
This is the port propeller, which was knocked out of position when it crashed on the seabed.

The starboard propeller, like the port propeller, is 23.5 ft (7 m) in diameter.

The fourth funnel was used for ventilation.

The ship's funnels
Three of the funnels took smoke from the boilers, but the fourth funnel was a fake to make the ship look more impressive.

The central propeller had four blades and was 16.5 ft (5 m) in diameter.

The port and starboard propellers had three blades.

The turbine shaft was 20.5 in (52 cm) in diameter.

There were two main condensers in the turbine room.

The turbine engine was in an iron casing, and weighed about 463 tons (420 tonnes).

Turbine engine room

Reciprocating engine room

Engine cylinders

Boiler room 1 contained five single-ended boilers.

How much fuel?

The amount of energy generated by a fuel is called its higher heating value and is measured in joules. The lower heating value is the amount of energy the fuel *actually* produces and depends on the efficiency of the engine in which the fuel is being used, and how much energy is lost due to evaporation and impurities.

TASK 1

If the higher heating value of coal is 27,216 million joules per ton (30,000 million joules per tonne) and the lower heating value of the coal on board the *Titanic* was ten percent of the higher heating value, figure out approximately how much coal the *Titanic* needed at the start of the journey.

TIP
Before the *Titanic* set sail it was estimated that she needed to produce approximately 18,000,000 million joules of energy to reach New York. When you do your calculations remember that one million = 1,000,000.

Colossal cylinders

The *Titanic*'s reciprocating engines were the largest ever built – over 30 ft (9 m) high. Each engine had four cylinders through which steam passed.

Keeping it going

Seventy-three trimmers and 177 firemen worked in the boiler rooms. Trimmers broke up coal into small lumps for the firemen to load into the boiler furnaces.

The circular doors on the boilers led to furnaces – there were a total of 159.

Boilers

The *Titanic* had 29 boilers, each over 16.5 ft (5 m) high. All 24 double-ended boilers are still within the bow section. The five single-ended ones are scattered around the debris field.

Excess steam could be released from the safety valves on either side of the funnels.

The uptakes led to the funnels.

Boiler rooms 2 to 5 each contained five double-ended boilers.

Coal bunker

The boilers were housed in watertight compartments.

The steam was carried to the engine rooms via steel pipes.

Smoke and waste gases were fed away from boilers through the uptakes.

Boiler room 6 contained four double-ended boilers.

Disaster Strikes

Inside *Nautile* the temperature has dropped to 35.6° F (2° C), the same as the water outside, so you may be feeling the cold. However, on the night of April 14, 1912, the sea temperature was even colder – it was below freezing. There was no trace of a wind, the sea was calm, and although the moon was not visible, there were many stars. As we move around the wreck, I will tell you more about the night of the disaster.

Icy waters

During her voyage, the *Titanic* received many ice warnings from other ships in the North Atlantic and as a precaution she took a course some 16 miles (26 km) south of the normal route. However, she did not slow down. On the night of the disaster she was traveling quite fast – about 20.5 knots (24 mph/38 kph).

Ship's light

Foremast

Bell

Warning lamp

This is the remains of the ship's mast light. High up on the foremast, it showed other ships which way the *Titanic* was traveling.

The crow's-nest was 50 ft (15 m) above the deck.

The crow's-nest

On the fallen foremast you can just make out the crow's-nest. In 1912 the crow's-nest contained a bell and a telephone for contacting the ship's bridge, and two people kept a constant lookout for icebergs and other ships.

The lookouts reached the crow's-nest via a ladder inside the foremast.

Lookout's bell

At 11:40 p.m. on April 14, 1912, Lookout Frederick Fleet saw an iceberg. He rang this bell, picked up the phone, and said "Iceberg right ahead."

Officers on the bridge were steering the ship.

HITTING THE ICEBERG

The alert from the lookout came too late for the *Titanic* to avoid the iceberg and it scraped along the starboard side of the ship. Although most of the passengers and crew felt only a slight jar, underwater the iceberg was creating a 300-ft (91-m) split in the *Titanic*'s hull.

The ice field
This is an artist's impression of the ice field into which the *Titanic* was sailing. It was over 6 miles (10 km) wide.

The iceberg seemed to have a scar of paint along it.

Atlantic iceberg
The day after the disaster, this iceberg was spotted near where the *Titanic* sank. It was between 50 and 100 ft (15 and 30 m) high.

Ice in the Atlantic
Ice was not unusual at these latitudes in April. The *Titanic* had actually received six warnings from other ships, and the men in the crow's-nest had been specifically told to keep a sharp lookout for icebergs. But it was not working practice to slow down until ice was actually spotted.

Artist's impression of the *Titanic* hitting the iceberg

EXPLORER'S TASK (G)

The size of an iceberg
Icebergs in the Atlantic Ocean are formed when huge chunks of ice break away from ice sheets and glaciers. Only one-ninth of the iceberg shows above water, the other eight-ninths are hidden below the water. This is because when water freezes it expands, causing the weight of the water the iceberg displaces to be more than the weight of the ice itself.

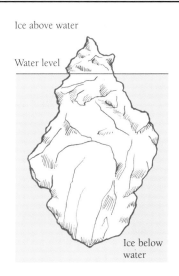

Ice above water

Water level

Ice below water

TASK 1
Using the diagram, figure out the volume of ice below the water if the volume of ice seen above water is 441,375 cubic ft (12,500 cubic meters).

TASK 2
Now that you have calculated the volume of the ice below the water, figure out the total volume of the iceberg.

TIP
Remember that only one-ninth of the iceberg is visible above the water.

"CQD – Sinking Fast!"

■ We are now moving around the area where the *Titanic*'s bridge once stood. This was the control center, where the captain and officers steered the ship, ordered the speed of its engines, and plotted its course. Imagine the scene on the bridge when the iceberg hit the ship, water started flooding in, and the captain and officers quickly had to decide on the best action to take.

ICE AHEAD

On hearing that there was an iceberg ahead, First Officer Murdoch ordered the engines to be stopped and put in reverse. He also ordered the wheel to be turned "Hard a' starboard." Although this steered the ship away from the iceberg, it was not quick enough to avoid a collision.

The bridge

Captain Smith rushed to the bridge as soon as he felt the collision. Now the bridge is almost unrecognizable. Only the base of the wheelhouse, and the telemotor to which the steering wheel was attached, mark the spot.

The iceberg scraped along the starboard side of the ship.

CUTAWAY OF THE *TITANIC* SHOWING THE FLOODING CAUSED BY THE ICEBERG

The ship's wireless (radio) was operated in the Marconi room by two employees of the Marconi Company.

The bridge contained telegraphs to communicate with the engine rooms.

First Officer Murdoch

Wheelhouse

At the time of the disaster there were five men on duty on the bridge.

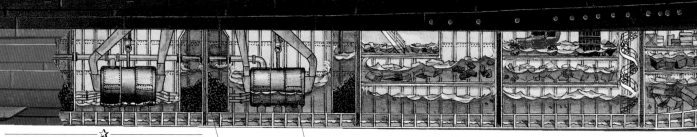

☆
TITANIC MYSTERY

Murdoch's actions nearly saved the ship. If the iceberg had been spotted a few seconds earlier, the disaster could have been avoided. So why were the lookouts not given binoculars, even though the ship was carrying them?

The bulkhead between boiler rooms 5 and 6 gave way at about 12:45 a.m.

If the first four compartments had flooded, rather than the first five, the ship would not have sunk.

The big leak

By 12:00 a.m. Captain Smith knew that, as the weight of the water in the compartments pulled the bow of the ship downward, the water would flow over the top of the compartments.

Morse code

Morse code is a set of dots, dashes, and spaces that can be sent, via an electric current, to the headset of an operator who translates the message. The process is instantaneous, which means Morse code messages can be received as they are being sent.

Morse code

a ●▬
b ▬●●●
c ▬●▬●
d ▬●●
e ●
f ●●▬●
g ▬▬●
h ●●●●
i ●●
j ●▬▬▬
k ▬●▬
l ●▬●●
m ▬▬
n ▬●
o ▬▬▬
p ●▬▬●
q ▬▬●▬
r ●▬●
s ●●●
t ▬
u ●●▬
v ●●●▬
w ●▬▬
x ▬●●▬
y ▬●▬▬
z ▬▬●●

TASK 1
Translate the following phrase into Morse code:
a) Struck iceberg, sinking fast

TASK 1
Use the Morse code to decipher the three following messages:

a) ▬●▬● ▬▬●▬ ▬●●
b) ●●● ▬▬▬ ●●●
c) ▬ ●● ▬ ●▬ ▬● ●● ▬●▬●

Marconi men
In 1912 all wireless communication was through Morse code. Just after midnight the *Titanic*'s two wireless operators were both in the Marconi room when Captain Smith told them to put out a distress call.

The Marconi operators used Morse code to send their messages.

Danger signals
The letters "CQ" were the traditional distress signal. By adding a "D" the signal meant that assistance was needed. The Marconi room used this signal until one of the operators remembered the new signal "SOS." The *Titanic* was the first liner ever to transmit this signal.

View of the bridge
The *Titanic*'s bridge contained telephones for contacting the rest of the ship, alarm bells, the control for closing the watertight doors, and telegraphs connected to the engine room. The ship's speed was controlled by officers on the bridge, who sent orders to the engine room via the telegraphs.

A telegraph
This telegraph, lying on the seabed, is from the docking bridge at the stern of the *Titanic*.

"MGY" was the *Titanic*'s call sign.

Watertight doors
The hull was divided by bulkheads into 16 compartments. Access between them was through the watertight doors. On the night of the disaster, although the doors were closed, the bulkheads were not high enough to prevent water from flowing over the top, from one compartment to the next.

The bulkheads were supposed to contain any leaks, but the water flowed over the top of them.

The post office, directly above the mail room, started to flood at 11:55 p.m.

This message was picked up by a ship called the *Carpathia*, which was over 58 miles (93 km) away from the *Titanic*.

Women and Children First

■ We are now just above the *Titanic*'s boat deck. All that remains are a few of the davits that were used to lower the lifeboats on the night of the disaster. This is one of the saddest places on the wreck – the sinking of the ship was one of the worst ever maritime disasters because there were not enough lifeboats for everyone to escape. Over two-thirds of the people on board the *Titanic* died on that terrible night.

Lifeboat davit

The British Board of Trade regulations required the *Titanic* to carry at least 16 lifeboats. Although the White Star Line exceeded these regulations by four, the *Titanic* could easily have carried far more lifeboats on the cleverly designed davits, which were capable of carrying more than one lifeboat each.

This davit was used to lower a lifeboat into the water.

Evacuation procedure

Soon after midnight, Captain Smith gave the order to prepare the lifeboats. He said that the women and children should evacuate the *Titanic* before the men. The first lifeboat touched the water at 12:25 a.m. on April 15, 1912. It carried less than half of its capacity of 65.

Captain Smith probably expected the half-empty lifeboats to come back to pick up people in the water. Unfortunately only one did.

AN OVERHEAD VIEW OF THE *TITANIC*'S DECKS

The lifeboats could hold a maximum of 65 people.

False safety

At first, few passengers believed that the *Titanic* was really sinking. On such a cold night, people were afraid of being lowered in an open boat 60 ft (18 m) down to the water below. During the evacuation, the crew had difficulty persuading people to get into the lifeboats.

Emergency plan

This plan shows the number of evacuation boats available. There were 14 lifeboats, two emergency boats, and four collapsible boats.

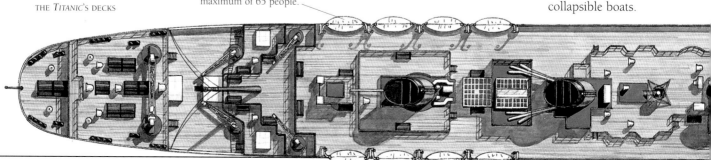

Going down
The *Titanic* finally sank at 2:20 a.m. on April 15, 1912. As her bow dipped underwater there were still many people huddled on her rising stern. Finally, the stern rose almost straight up and slid under the water.

THE RESCUE
The *Titanic*'s distress messages were picked up by many ships in the area. All steamed toward the *Titanic*, but none reached her before she sank. The *Carpathia* arrived first. At 4:10 a.m. her crew started to pick up the survivors, and by 8 a.m. they were all safely on board.

The "life jacket"
There were enough life jackets for the passengers and crew, but they gave no protection against the freezing sea. Most people died of the cold, not by drowning.

☆
TITANIC MYSTERY

As the *Titanic* was sinking, officers saw a ship about five or six miles away. They tried to signal with a Morse lamp, but the ship vanished. Who was she and why did she ignore the *Titanic*?

The collapsible boats could hold a maximum of 47 people.

The emergency boats could hold a maximum of 40 people.

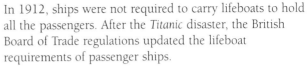
Chance of survival
In 1912, ships were not required to carry lifeboats to hold all the passengers. After the *Titanic* disaster, the British Board of Trade regulations updated the lifeboat requirements of passenger ships.

Boats on board the *Titanic*

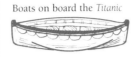

14 lifeboats
2 emergency boats
4 collapsible boats

Source for victims/survivors: the British Inquiry

TASK 1
The lifeboats could hold 65 people each, the emergency boats 40 people each, and the collapsible boats 47 people each. Figure out how many passengers and crew could have left the *Titanic* safely.

TASK 2
There were 2,206 passengers and crew on board the *Titanic*. What percentage of them had a chance of getting into a lifeboat?

TASK 3
1,503 people died when the *Titanic* sank. How many died because the lifeboats were not full?

Bruce Ismay sent this message from the *Carpathia* to International Mercantile Marine, the owners of the White Star Line.

Unlucky escape
Bruce Ismay, White Star Line chairman, was a passenger on the *Titanic*. He helped load the lifeboats, but by getting into one himself he ruined his reputation, unlike Captain Smith, who went down with his ship.

Collapsible boat D
This was the last lifeboat to leave the *Titanic* and it reached the *Carpathia* at 7 a.m. Its passengers had spent nearly five hours waiting to be rescued.

Survivors on the *Carpathia*
The *Carpathia* had been on her way from New York to Gibraltar. Now she headed back to New York.

Touring the Seabed

"Hello. I'm Diana Barton, the conservator on board the *Nadir*. I'll be advising you, through *Nautile's* underwater telephone, on how to recover objects from the seabed for an exhibition."

■ We are now approaching the debris field. When the *Titanic* sank, she broke in half and a great many objects, large and small, tumbled out and floated down to the bottom of the ocean. Over the years, some of the objects have disappeared, some have deteriorated, and some are still in perfect condition. The remaining debris now lies scattered over the seabed to the south of the stern.

THE DEBRIS FIELD

Most objects are lying on top of the seabed, but because there is a current, some of the small items may have been covered by silt. You will not see much life here. There are a few fish, crabs, and shrimps living off algae, but plants cannot exist because there is no light.

Rat-tailed fish can be seen swimming around the wreck.

Debris spotting
The only visual aids you have are the lights on the front of *Nautile*, so you need a mixture of careful observation and good luck to help you find objects.

The "rusticles" break off if touched by *Nautile*.

Glazed objects
Many of the delicate glass and china objects are undamaged. These items came to rest gently on the silt on the seabed.

The wooden crates have been eaten away, leaving the dishes perfectly stacked.

Iron age
You will notice that the ship is covered with rust that looks like icicles. These are called "rusticles" and are formed by iron-eating bacteria. "Rusticles" grow until they fall off under their own weight.

Wood borers
These ceramic dishes probably fell to the seabed in a wooden packing crate. All the soft wood was eaten away by wood-boring mollusks years ago.

Well dressed

Most clothing would have disintegrated during the first few years on the seabed. In some cases, however, shoes have survived. Leather is more resilient than cotton and wool.

Records of the past

Many of the objects give a uniquely detailed insight into the world of 1912. This letter was completely black when it was found on the seabed. It was restored in a laboratory and is now readable.

The letter comments on the fashion of wearing a feather boa.

Artifacts that have been immersed in seawater for years are porous and fragile and must be handled with care.

Bench mark

This frame from a deck bench is made of cast bronze and its years underwater have not caused any serious damage. However, it has absorbed chlorides and sulfides from the water, which have weakened and stained it.

HELPING HAND

The pressure of the water outside *Nautile* is so great it is impossible for you to leave the safety of the submersible. You must rely on *Nautile's* articulated (jointed) arms, and their special tool attachments, to place objects from the debris field into the lifting baskets.

Nautile's pilot operates the arms from inside the submersible.

Heavy load

This heavy safe is virtually weightless underwater. *Nautile's* arms use the clamp attachments to grip the awkward shape.

This plate is being picked up with the sucker attachment.

Delicate touch

Nautile's arms have several attachments, a shovel, a sucker, and a gripper, for picking up delicate objects.

Nautile's arm can grip china without breaking it.

★ EXPLORER'S TASK **J**

Preservation of objects

At the bottom of the sea it is cold, there is no light, and the oxygen levels are low. These conditions slow down deterioration, but objects still suffer varying degrees of damage. Different materials deteriorate at different rates:

- Soft organic material, such as food, clothing, and wood, is at the greatest risk from fish and bacteria
- Marine worms bore holes in anything wooden
- Inorganic material, such as metal, ceramic, and glass, deteriorates more slowly, but it, too, is under threat
- Steel and iron are weakened by bacteria, but bronze objects are hardly affected
- Glass survives best of all

TASK 1

Using the information provided, list the following items in the order in which you would expect them to deteriorate. Start with the item that would deteriorate most quickly.

a) a champagne bottle   b) a loaf of bread
c) a solid bronze bench frame   d) a wooden shelf

Returning to the *Nadir*

It is time to return to the surface. *Nautile* will drop her weights – the bags of steel shot – and you will start to rise gently through the water. An hour and a half later, you will notice the water get lighter and lighter, until finally you reach the surface. There, the objects you placed in the lifting baskets will have already been raised and taken on board the *Nadir*, ready for you to record and clean them.

SURFACING IN *NAUTILE*

The *Nadir* monitors *Nautile's* position as she rises. Just before *Nautile* breaks the surface, a diving team is sent out in an inflatable boat. Their job is to fasten ropes to *Nautile* so that she can be guided toward the *Nadir*.

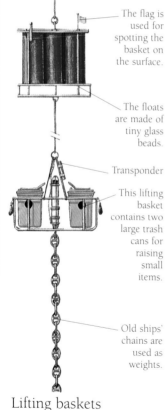

The flag is used for spotting the basket on the surface.

The floats are made of tiny glass beads.

Transponder

This lifting basket contains two large trash cans for raising small items.

Old ships' chains are used as weights.

Lifting baskets
To raise the baskets from the seabed, a signal is sent to the transponder from the *Nadir*. This signal activates a mechanism on the basket that releases the chain weights so that the baskets slowly float up to the surface of the ocean.

Landing history
The lifting baskets are raised and pulled back on board the *Nadir* while *Nautile* is still on the seabed. This is to prevent any possible collisions or entanglements between them.

This is one of the open lifting baskets used to raise larger objects.

Back to mother
The most difficult part of the whole operation is when the *Nadir* lifts *Nautile* out of the water. You cannot leave *Nautile* until she is safely secured on the deck of the *Nadir*.

Emptying the baskets
The baskets are unloaded on the stern of the *Nadir* and the objects carried to the conservation laboratory on board. Smaller objects are wrapped in foam or bubble wrap and stored in trays for the voyage home.

The team will make special carrying frames for the larger objects, like this deck bench.

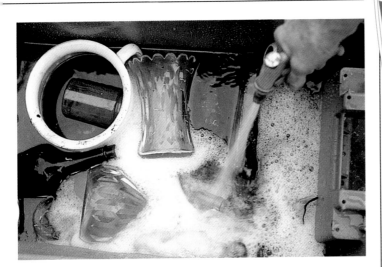

Hosing down
A large amount of mud is always brought up from the seabed with the basket. The mud is quite acidic and very smelly, but a high-pressure hose, which uses some of the *Nadir's* valuable freshwater supply, is used to take off the worst of it.

Washing up
It is vital to keep objects immersed in water or they will start to deteriorate. It is also important to wash away the salts that have penetrated the objects.

Security check
On your return you will be asked for a list of all the objects you saw being picked up from the seabed. It will be checked with a list of everything that arrived on the *Nadir*. This way, there is no possibility of anything going missing.

All the items can be checked again with the video footage of the dive.

Surviving on the seabed
At sea level the pressure of the atmosphere around us is relatively constant. The deeper you go underwater, the higher the pressure level becomes. The pressure pushes in on flexible air spaces, compressing them and reducing their volume. The air is not lost, it is simply compressed.

TASK 1
A number of champagne bottles sank with the *Titanic*. As they fell, air inside the bottles, in between the champagne and the cork, was compressed by the pressure of the water outside. When the wreck was found 76 years later, what do you think the champagne bottles looked like when they were raised?

a) the corks had been pushed inside the bottles
b) the bottles had exploded
c) the corks had been pushed out of the bottles
d) the corks were intact

PRESERVING THE PAST
Before the objects can be displayed in an exhibition they must be cleaned up. Much of this work uses dangerous chemicals, which could easily spill on a ship at sea. So the full conservation treatment will take place in a laboratory on dry land.

Salty cherub
The green streaks on this bronze cherub are a product of corrosion. The cherub must be treated to make its condition stable or it will deteriorate rapidly.

Surface salts are simply washed out using freshwater.

Electrolysis treatment
Removing the salts trapped inside the cherub is difficult. It is done by connecting the cherub to a power supply and placing it in a chemical bath lined with a stainless steel grid. The salts are attracted to the current, so as the current passes from the cherub to the grid, it takes the salts along with it.

Salt water reacts with bronze to create a corrosive green coating called verdigris.

The Legend Lives On

■ Now that you are back on dry land and the objects that you recovered have been properly conserved, they will become part of a public exhibition. The exhibition will tell the story of the *Titanic* and her passengers, and also give a glimpse of the world in 1912. The *Titanic* continues to fascinate people, and many books, paintings, documentaries, and movies have been created to tell its tragic story.

MIXED VIEWS

Some people disliked the idea of recovering objects from the wreck because they felt it should be left alone out of respect for those who died. Others believe that having objects from the wreck on display can help teach present and future generations about the lessons to be learned from this maritime tragedy.

Style baby

This cherub was part of the first-class aft grand staircase. It is a late-17th-century English decorative style.

Winning seat

A deck bench frame can been refitted with wooden seating to show it as it would have looked on a White Star Line ship.

Painted ships

There are many paintings of the *Titanic*. Artists have tried to capture her maiden voyage and the events of the disaster.

Running water

In 1912 many of the *Titanic's* passengers would not have had running water in their homes. These taps are a symbol of the on-board luxury.

This Gladstone bag contained a large amount of money and pieces of jewelry.

A passenger's pipe

Porthole

A clever feature of the exhibition will allow people to look through this porthole, just as the passengers on the *Titanic* once did.

Personal possessions

Individual items are almost impossible to spot on the seabed. These small personal objects were recovered from a bag. They form an important part of the exhibition as they give us some insight into the lives of the people who owned them.

Gold chain and pendant

Spectacle case

Steel-rimmed spectacles

Waterman fountain pen

Plate from a
dining saloon

Beer bottle

Teapot

Silver fork

Class division
There were over 12,000 dinner
plates and 8,000 forks on the
Titanic. Displaying the dishware
and cutlery from the *Titanic* is a
good way of showing the strict
class structure on the ship –
there was a different type of
dinner plate for each class.

Gratin dishes
There is no better
way to display
these dishes than
stacked as you
found them on
the seabed.

Past or present
This is what remains
of one of the light
fixtures from the first-
class staircase. You can
see that the *Titanic* used
lightbulbs just like those
we use today.

Socket for
lightbulb

Ship shape
Some of the ship's
equipment, such as a
bell, a telegraph, and a
lifeboat davit, have
been raised from the
seabed. By displaying
these items people
who come to the
exhibition get a good
idea of what an
enormous ship the
Titanic was.

Telegraph
from the
docking
bridge

WHY DID IT HAPPEN?
Should the *Titanic* have sailed more slowly? Should
she have had more lifeboats? Should she have been
better designed? All these issues were discussed in
the inquiry that followed the disaster. Once the
wreck was found, at least the reason why the ship
broke up was explained.

How the ship broke up
1. The compartments flood as
water begins to flow from
one to another over the top
of the bulkheads.

2. The weight of the water pulls
the bow under and the first
funnel collapses. The water
crushes the glass dome at the
top of the Grand Staircase.

3. The water in the forward part
of the ship pulls the ship down so
much that the stern rises out of
the water to about 45°. This puts
a huge strain on the hull.

4. Not designed to take such a
strain, the ship snaps in two. The
stern lowers and the funnels all
break free.

5. As the bow glides away, some of
the contents of the ship, including
the single-ended boilers, spill out.
The stern starts to flood.

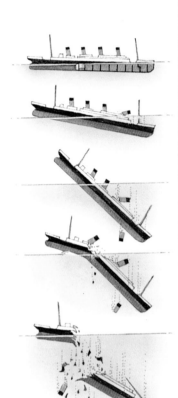

To the seabed
Once the *Titanic* had broken in two, the
bow section fell gently down, nose first,
until it hit the mud on the seabed. The
stern section tipped up until it was almost vertical
in the water, then it slipped under the surface and
fell horizontally to the bottom of the ocean.

Spreading the news
Look in your local library for
reprints of newspapers from
April 1912, and you can see
for yourself how the news
broke. At first it was
thought that everyone
had been rescued, but
as the days passed, the
tragic details emerged.

ST. LOUIS POST-DISPATCH
1302 LIVES LOST WHEN "TITANIC" SANK; 868 SAVED
Carpathia Steaming to New York With Survivors; None on Other Ships
HOME EDITION

7 ST. LOUISANS ARE
REPORTED SAFE ON
BOARD CARPATHIA

2-THIRDS WOMEN
IN PARTIAL LIST
OF THOSE RESCUED

This newspaper
underestimated
the tragedy.

Index

Picture credits
Every effort has been made to trace the copyright holders. DK apologizes for any unintentional omissions and would be pleased, in such cases, to add an acknowledgment in future editions. The publisher would like to thank the following individuals, companies, and picture libraries for their kind permission to reproduce their photographs:
Mary Evans Picture Library: 19cr, 23crb, c, 29br; The Hulton Getty Picture Collection Ltd: 22cl, cr; Ifremer: 11cla, c, 31c; Illustrated London News: 19cl; The Irish Picture Library: 21cr, br, tl F.R. Browne Collection; MacQuitty International Collection: 12c, 14tr, 23cl, 25tr; Ken Marshall Collection: 15bc, 17c, 19clb; National Geographic: 6tr, 8br, 12tr, 13tc, 14bc, 16tr, 17tc, 18cl Emory Kristof; National Maritime Museum: 12bl, 13bc; Rex Features: 6cr, 14bc, br, 15tl, bc, br, 16cr, 18tr, bl, 21cb, 23tl, cr, 24br, 27bc, ca, bc, 28cl, tr, cr, bl, cb, 29ca, bc/11tc Nils Jorgansen/9tc R. Sobol; Frank Spooner Pictures: 4br, 9bl, 14bl, 18cr, 21c, 24clb, 26cra, 27cr, 29cl; Sygma: 9cl, 10tr, cr, 15bl, 20tr, 24cra, c, 25tc, cla, bl, cb, br, 26br, 27tl, ca, bl, 28br, 29tl, tc, cl; Ulster Folk & Transport Museum: 9tr, 13cl, 17c; Woods Hole Oceanographic Institute: 9tl. Jacket: Ken Marshall Collection: front cla; Ulster Folk & Transport Museum: front ca; National Maritime Museum: front bc; Sygma: front clb.

EXPLORER'S TASK ANSWERS

Acknowledgments
DK would like to thank the following people for their contributions to this book: Stephen Bull for the explorer's task illustrations, Paul Bampton and Eryl Davies for consultancy on the explorer's tasks, and Ryan Davis.